# Preface

In the vast expanse of the cosmos, few cultures have captivated the imagination as profoundly as the Klingons. Their way of life, rooted in honor, courage, and an unyielding warrior ethos, speaks to something primal and deeply respected. This book, "Voices of Qo'noS: The Wisdom of Klingons," is a bridge between worlds – an invitation to understand the heart and soul of a people both feared and admired.

For the student of Klingon culture, whether born of Earth or Qo'noS, this text offers more than mere translations. It is a journey into the philosophy and spirit of the Klingon people. Each phrase, presented in its original Klingon script **plqaD**, its romanized form, and translated into English, serves as a window into the complex Klingon way of life.

Klingon proverbs are not just words; they are echoes of a history forged in the fires of countless battles, a testament to a people who see life and death, joy and sorrow, strength and weakness, through a lens unlike any other. These phrases are the beating heart of Klingon culture, offering guidance, wisdom, and insight into their way of life.

To those embarking on this exploration, be it out of academic interest, personal growth, or a deeper understanding of a friend or foe, know this: the words within these pages are more than mere sentences. They are the breath and blood of a proud, fierce, and noble race. They teach us about honor, loyalty, strength, and the importance of living with courage and conviction.

As you turn these pages, let each proverb challenge you, inspire you, and provide a deeper understanding of the Klingon spirit. Embrace the journey, and may you find your own strength and honor reflected in the wisdom of the Klingons.

Qapla'!

# KLINGON TEACHINGS

## Warrior ethos

Many proverbs emphasize the importance of being a warrior. Phrases like "Klingons are born, live as warriors, then die" and "A warrior's blood boils before the fire is hot" suggest a culture deeply rooted in the ideals of warfare, bravery, and combat prowess.

## Honor and pride

Honor is a recurring theme. Proverbs like "There is nothing shameful in falling before a superior enemy" and "There is no honor in attacking the weak" indicate a strong sense of honor and fairness in combat. Pride in their race and actions, as shown in "Klingons are a proud race, and we intend to go on being proud", is also significant.

## Action and Decisiveness

Klingons value action and decisiveness. Sayings like "If you are sad, act!" and "Klingons do not procrastinate" suggest a preference for direct action over contemplation or delay.

## Strength and Courage

Physical and moral strength are prized. "Brute strength is not the most important asset in a fight" implies a respect for inner strength and courage over mere physical power.

## Survival and Expansion

The importance of survival and expansion is evident in phrases like "To survive, we must expand." This shows a focus on growth and the sustenance of their people and way of life.

## Companionship and Loyalty

The value placed on not abandoning friends in battle and the emphasis on communal identity, as in "One is always of his tribe", highlight a strong sense of loyalty and the importance of the group over the individual.

## Family and Legacy

Klingon culture places great importance on family and ancestry. Phrases like "The dishonor of the father dishonors his sons and their sons for three generations" suggest a collective sense of honor and responsibility within families.

## Endurance and Resilience

The Klingons' disdain for comfort and pleasure, as seen in "Pleasure is nonessential" and "A warrior does not complain about physical discomfort", reflects a culture that values endurance, resilience, and the ability to withstand hardship.

## Directness and Honesty

A straightforward approach to life is evident in "Klingons never bluff" and the emphasis on action over words. This suggests a culture that values honesty and directness.

## Spiritual and Ancestral Connection

References to blood and ancestors, such as "Listen to the voice of your blood" and "The memory of you sings in my blood", indicate a deep spiritual connection to their lineage and ancestors.

## Valor and Courage

Sayings like "A beard is a symbol of courage" and "A warrior fights to the death" emphasize a deep-seated valor among Klingons. Courage is not just valued but seen as a defining characteristic of their identity.

## Personal Responsibility and Accountability

The emphasis on personal responsibility is clear in sayings like "Have the courage to admit your mistakes" and "The family of a Klingon warrior is responsible for his actions, and he is responsible for theirs", highlighting a culture where individuals are accountable for their actions and their consequences.

## Fear and Caution

Contrary to a purely fearless image, proverbs like "Only fools have no fear" suggest a nuanced understanding of fear and caution as necessary for survival and wisdom.

## Skepticism and Trust

Klingons seem to value skepticism in dealing with others, as seen in "Don't trust those who frequently smile" and "Don't trust Ferengi who give back money." This suggests a culture that values vigilance and discernment in social interactions.

# If you are sad, act!

bl'IQchugh ylvang .

# Pleasure is nonessential

'utbe' bel

# understand life, endure pain.

yIn DayajmeH 'oy' yISIQ .

# A warrior does not complain about physical discomfort.

loQ 'oy'DI' SuvwI' bepbe' .

# Klingons do not procrastinate.

lumbe' tlhInganpu'.

# Klingons do not lie in bed.

QongDaqDaq Qotbe' tlhInganpu'.

# There is always a chance.

reH 'eb tu'lu' .

# Capture all opportunities.

Hoch 'ebmey tIjon .

Hit them hard and hit them fast.

tlqlppu' 'ej nom tlqlp .

# If it's in your way, knock it down.

Dubotchugh ylpummoH .

# Klingons are born, live as warriors, then die.

bogh tlhInganpu' ; SuvwI'pu' moj ; Hegh .

# We fight to enrich the spirit.

qa' wIje'meH maSuv .

# Klingons are born to fight and conquer.

SuvmeH 'ej charghmeH bogh tlhInganpu'.
________

# When threatened, fight.

DabuQlu'DI' yISuv .

# To survive, we must expand.

mataHmeH maSachnIS .

# Klingons are a proud race, and we intend to go on being proud.

Hem tlhIngan Segh 'ej maHemtaH 'e' wIHech .

# The memory of you sings in my blood.

bomDI' 'IwwIj qaqaw .

Choose to fight, not negotiate.
bISuv 'e' yIwIv bISutlh 'e' yIwIvQo'.

If you must negotiate, watch you enemy's eyes.

bISutlhnIS jaghlI' mInDu' tIbej .

# Great deeds, great songs.

ta'mey Dun ; bommey Dun .
___________

Real power is in the heart.
tlqDaq HoSna' tu'lu' .

# Brute strength is not the most important asset in a fight.

Suvlu'taHvIS yapbe' HoS neH .

# There is no honor in attacking the weak.

pujwI' HIvlu'chugh quvbe'lu' .

There is nothing shameful in falling before a superior enemy.

Dujeychugh jagh nIv yItuHQo'.

doubt, surprise them.

bISovbejbe'DI' tImer .

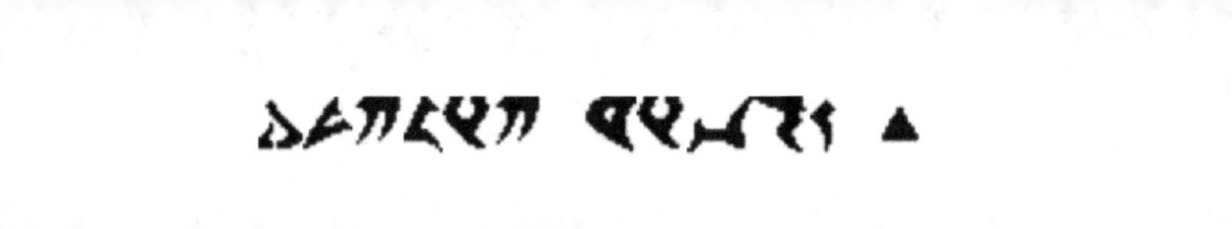

# Listen to the voice of your blood.

’Iwllj ghogh yIQoy .

# A warrior's blood boils before the fire is hot.

tujpa' qul pub SuvwI' 'Iw .

# Blood and water don't mix.

tay'taHbe' 'Iw bIQ je .

# There are no old warriors.

# In space, all warriors are cold warriors.

loghDaq Suvrupbogh Suvwl'pu' chaH Hoch Suvwl'pu''e' .

# Drinking fake ale is better than drinking water.

tlhutlhmeH HIq ngeb qaq law' bIQ qaq puS .

# A warrior does not let a friend face danger alone.

nIteb Qob qaD jup 'e' chaw'be' SuvwI' .

# When a warrior goes to battle, he does not abandon his friends.

may'Daq jaHDI' SuvwI' juppu'Daj lonbe' .

# Adhere to virtue honorably.

batlh ghob yIpab .
———

# Virtue is the reward.

# Honor is more important than life.

batlh potlh law' yIn potlh puS .

not toj tlhInganpu'.

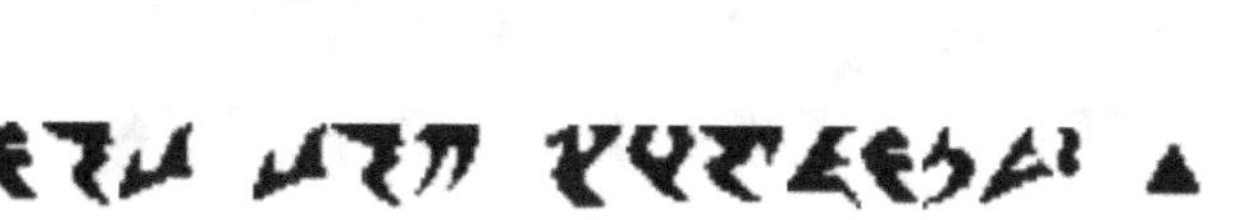

# No Klingon ever breaks his word.

not lay'Ha' tlhIngan .
___________

# When you insult a Klingon's honor, prepare for trouble.

tlhIngan quv DatIchDI' Seng yIghuH .

———

# The Klingon who kills without showing his face has no honor.

quv Hutlh HoHbogh tlhIngan 'ach qabDaj 'angbe'bogh .

# Have the courage to admit your mistakes

Qaghmeyllj tIchID ; ylyoH .

# A beard is a symbol of courage.

toDuj 'oS rol .

# Have the courage to admit your mistakes.

Qaghmeyllj tIchID ; ylyoH .
______

# Better to die on our feet than live on our knees.

QamvIS Hegh qaq law' torvIS yIn qaq puS .

# A warrior fights to the death.

wej Heghchugh vay' ; SuvtaH SuvwI' .

———

# Death is an experience best shared.

Heghlu'DI' mobbe'lu'chugh QaQpu'
Hegh wanI'.

———

# If you are afraid to die, you have already died.

bIHeghvIpchugh bIHeghpu'.

# Even the best blade will rust and grow dull unless it is cared for.

'etlh QorghHa'lu'chugh ragh 'etlh nIvqu' 'ej jejHa'choH .

# One is always of his tribe.

reH tay' ghot tuqDaj je .

# The family of a Klingon warrior is responsible for his actions, and he is responsible for theirs.

vangDI' tlhIngan SuvwI' ngoy' qorDu'Daj vangDI' qorDu'Daj ngoy' tlhIngan SuvwI'.

# The dishonor of the father dishonors his sons and their sons for three generations

qaStaHvIS wej puq poHmey vav
puqloDpu' puqloDpu'chaj
je quvHa'moH vav quvHa'ghach .

# Only fools have no fear.

not qoHpu’’e’ neH ghIjlu’.

vay' DaghIjlaHchugh bIHoSghaj .

---

# Always it is the brave ones who die.

reH Hegh yoHwI'pu''e' .

# Revenge is the best revenge.

bortaS nIvqu' 'oH bortaS'e'.

ylvoq 'ach yl'ol .
___________

# Trust, but locate the doors.

yIvoq 'ach lojmItmey yISam .

Don't trust Ferengi who give back money.

Huch nobHa'bogh verenganpu''
e' yIvoqQo'.

# Don't trust those who frequently smile.

plj monchugh vay' ylvoqQo'.

# Destroying an empire to win a war is no victory, and ending a battle to save an empire is no defeat.

noH QapmeH wo' Qaw'lu'chugh
yay chavbe'lu' 'ej wo'
choqmeH may' DoHlu'chugh lujbe'lu' .

# Closing remarks

As we reach the end of this book, it is my fervent hope that you, the reader, have not only gained a deeper understanding of Klingon culture but also found within these pages insights that resonate with your own life. The teachings and proverbs of the Klingon people, offer more than a glimpse into an alien way of life; they provide timeless wisdom that transcends the boundaries of worlds and species.

The values of the Klingons, though rooted in a culture far removed from many of ours, hold universal truths. Their emphasis on personal honor, accountability, and the importance of facing challenges with bravery and resilience are principles that can guide us in our daily lives. The lessons on family, loyalty, and the respect for both nature and tradition remind us of the enduring bonds and responsibilities that we all share, regardless of our origins.

As you implement these teachings in your own journey, remember that the spirit of the Klingon warrior is not about seeking conflict but about facing life with determination and strength. It is about standing up for what is right, even in the face of adversity, and about being true to oneself and one's values. The Klingon way teaches us to embrace life fully, to meet challenges head-on, and to always act with honor and courage.

Whether you are navigating the complexities of personal relationships, facing professional challenges, or simply seeking a path of personal growth, the wisdom of the Klingons can serve as a beacon. Let their proverbs inspire you to live with greater strength, honor, and bravery. Let their insights encourage you to face your fears, to stand firm in your convictions, and to always strive for personal and collective betterment.

In closing, may the wisdom of the Klingons enrich your spirit as it has enriched theirs. May you find in their words the courage to face the unknown, the strength to endure life's battles, and the honor to live a life of integrity and purpose.

Qapla'! (Success!)

# Brought to you by

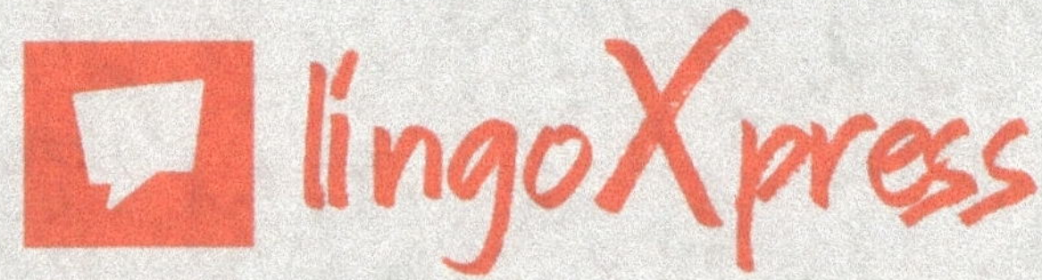